G!RRRL Power!

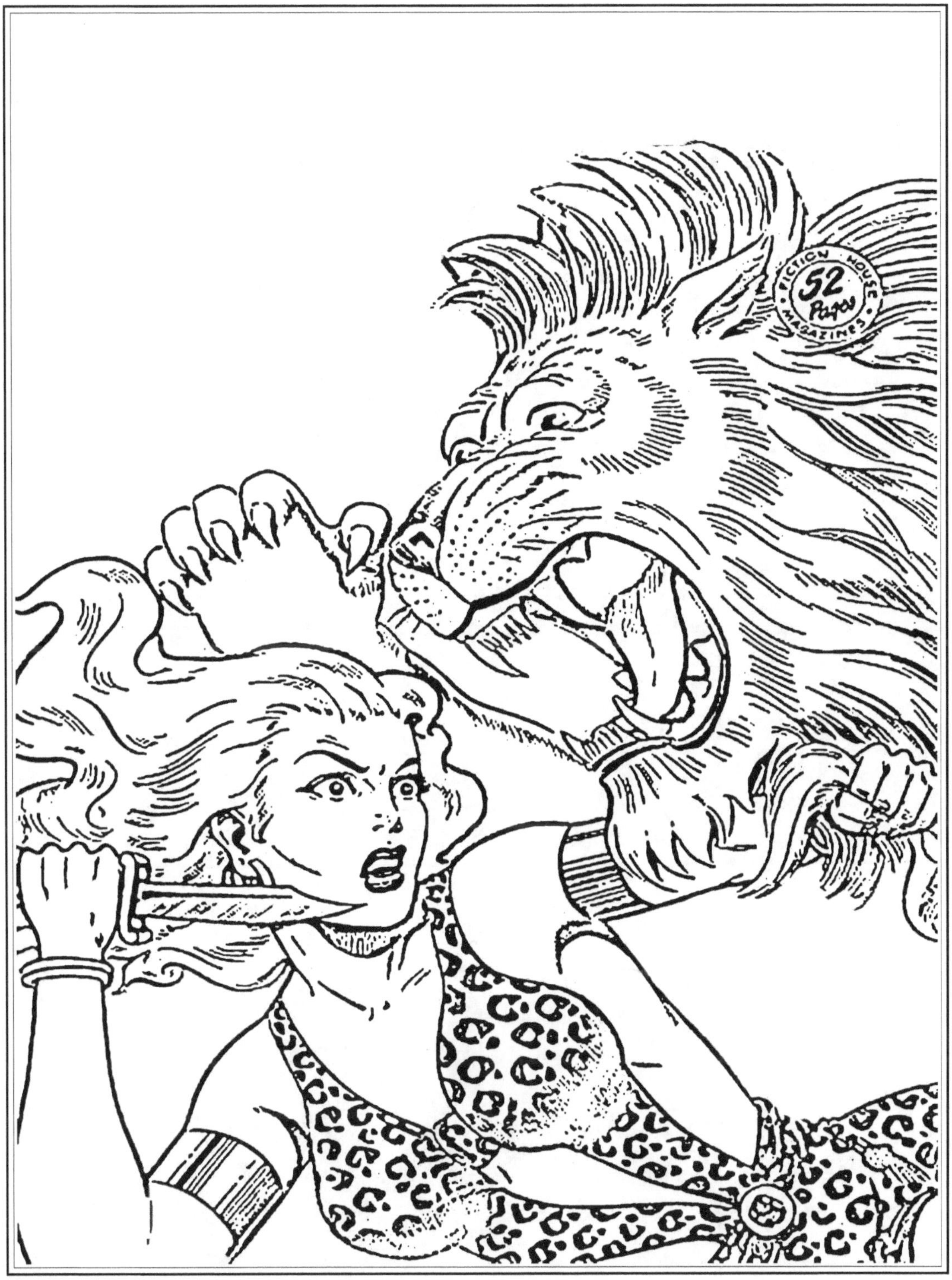

G!RRRL Power!

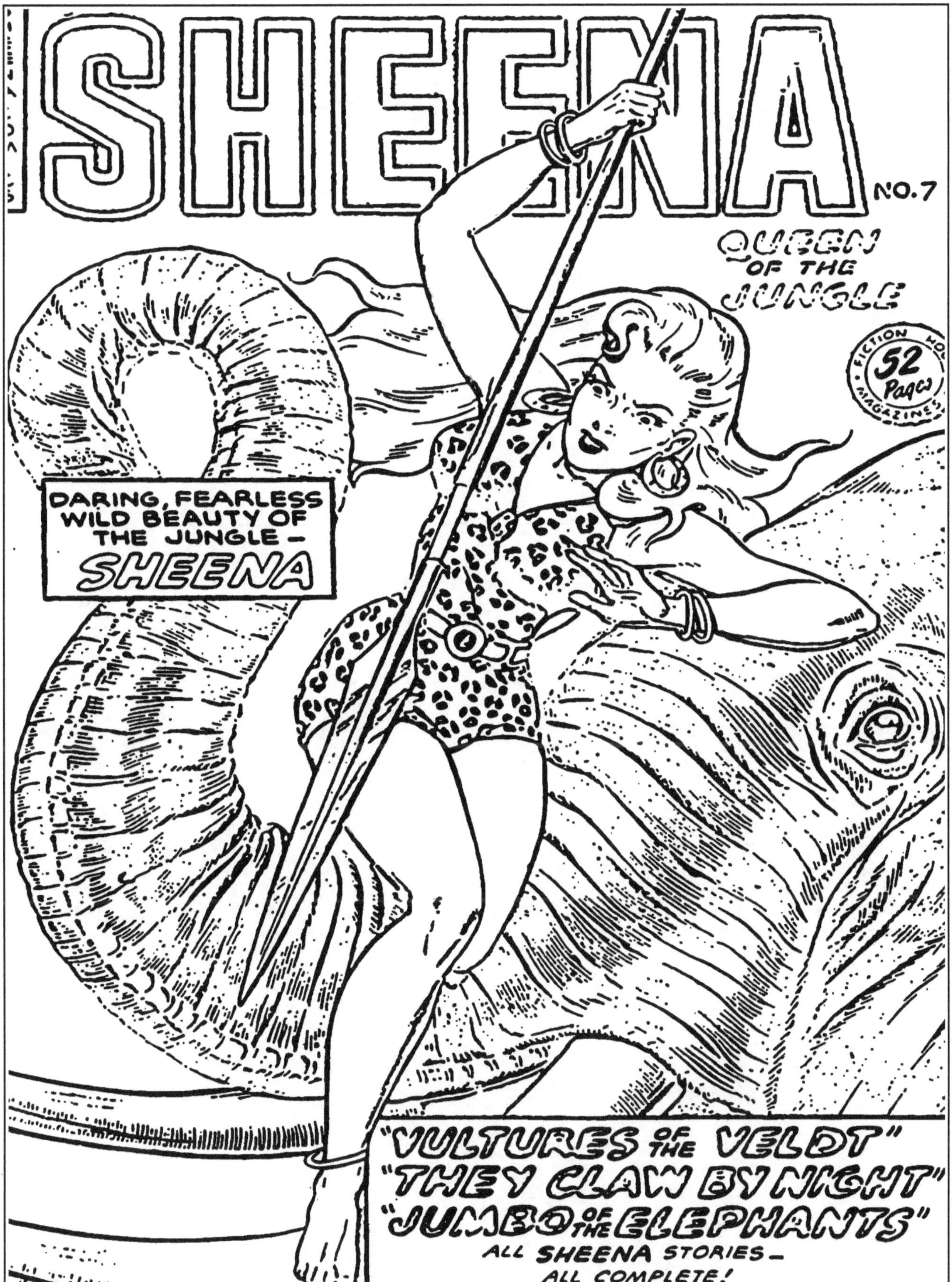
SHEENA
NO.7
QUEEN OF THE JUNGLE
FICTION HOUSE MAGAZINES
52 Pages
DARING, FEARLESS WILD BEAUTY OF THE JUNGLE – SHEENA
"VULTURES OF THE VELDT"
"THEY CLAW BY NIGHT"
"JUMBO OF THE ELEPHANTS"
ALL SHEENA STORIES – ALL COMPLETE!

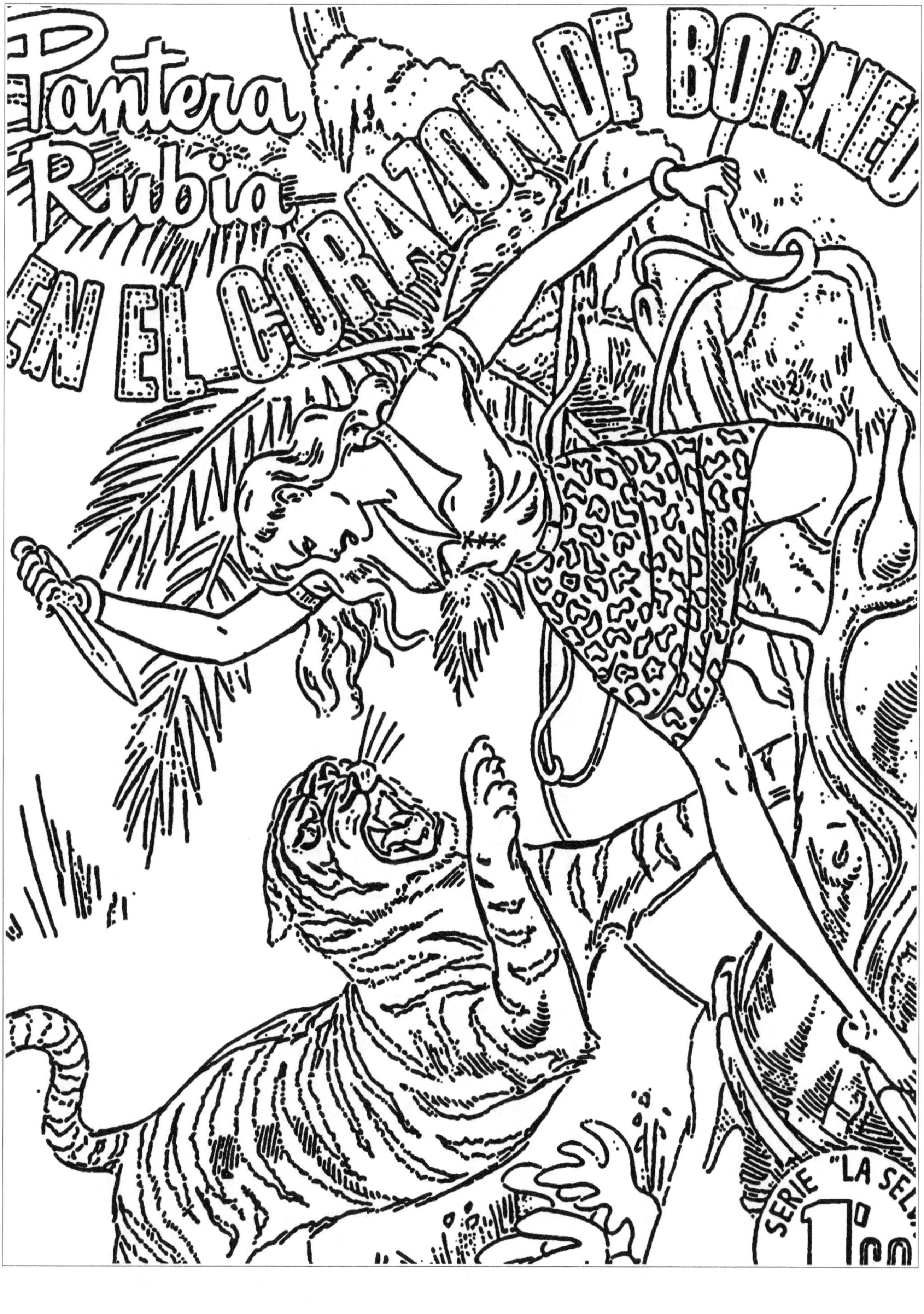
Pantera Rubia
EN EL CORAZON DE BORNEO
SERIE

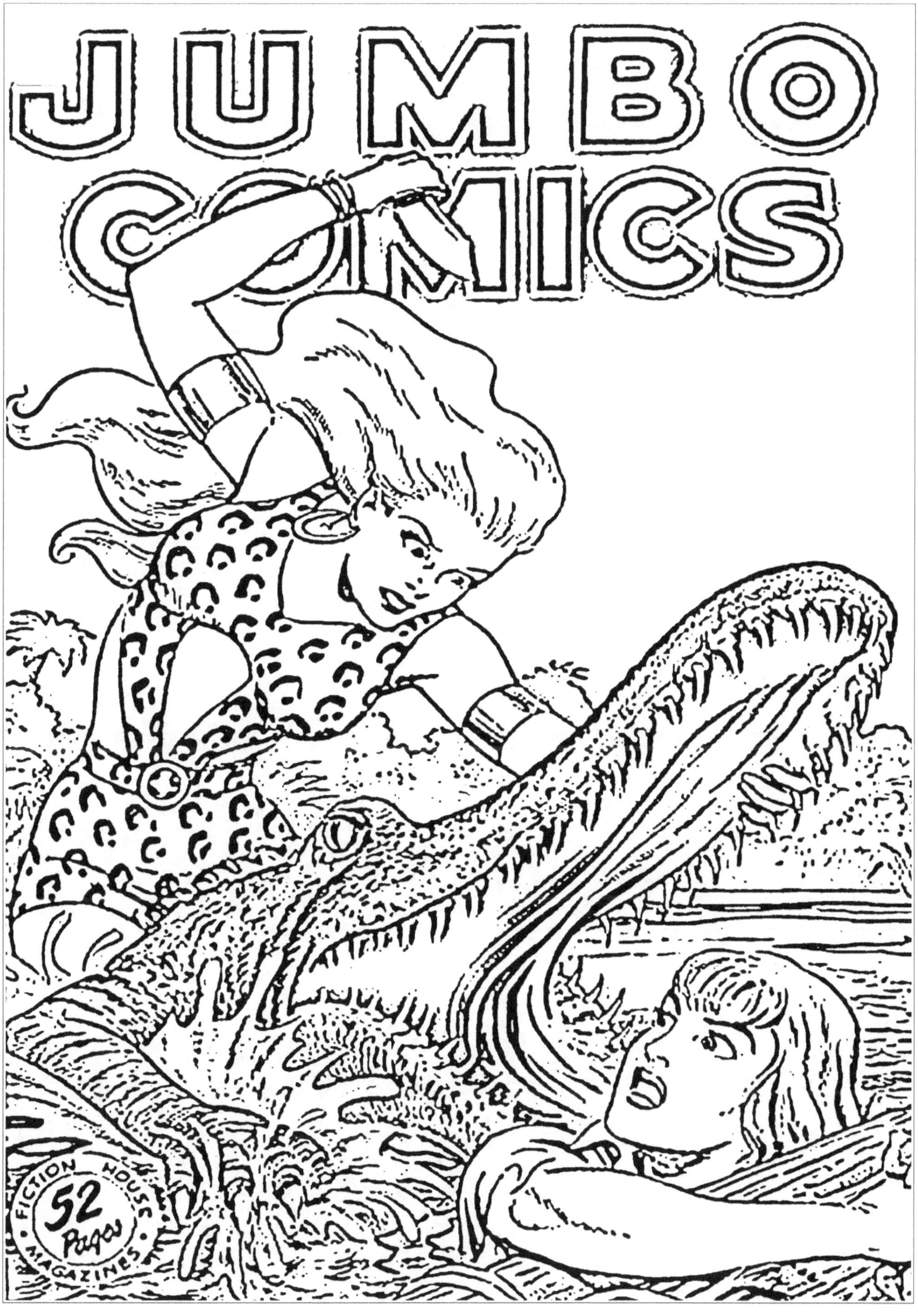
JUMBO
COMICS
FICTION HOUSE MAGAZINES
52 Pages

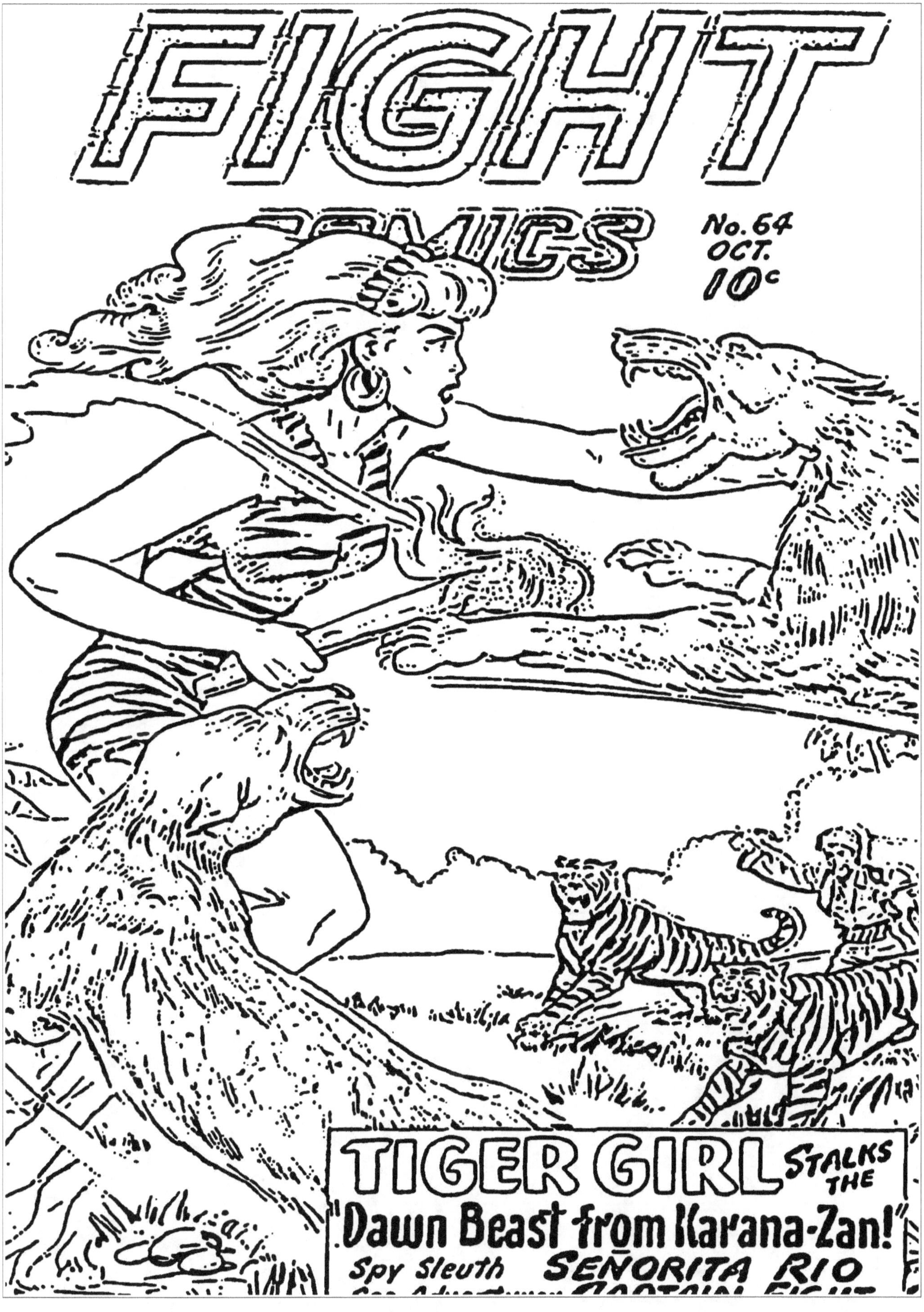
FIGHT
No. 64
OCT.
10c
TIGER GIRL
STALKS THE
"Dawn Beast from Karana-Zan!"
Spy Sleuth SEÑORITA RIO

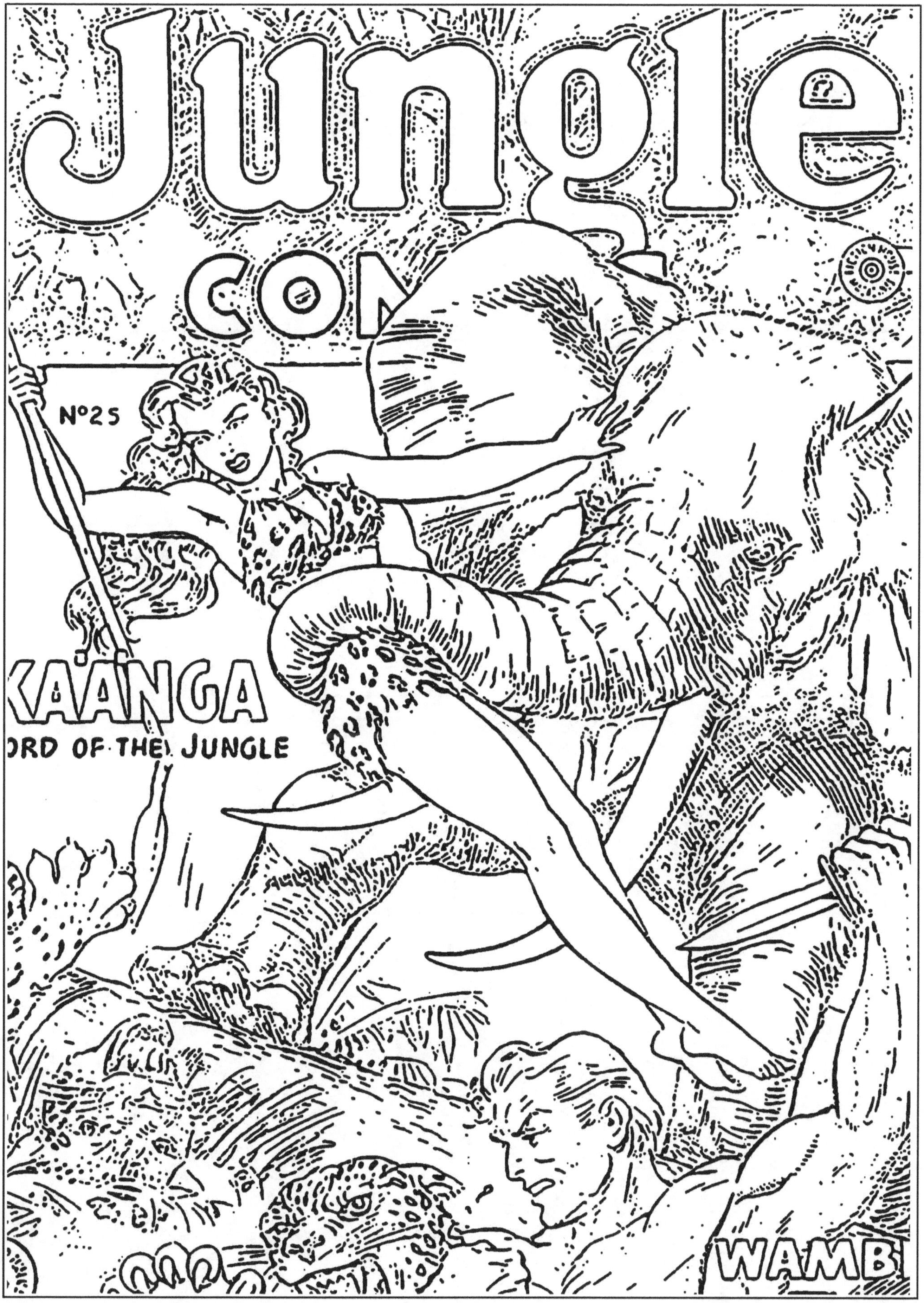

Jungle
COM
Nº25
KAANGA
ORD OF THE JUNGLE
WAMB

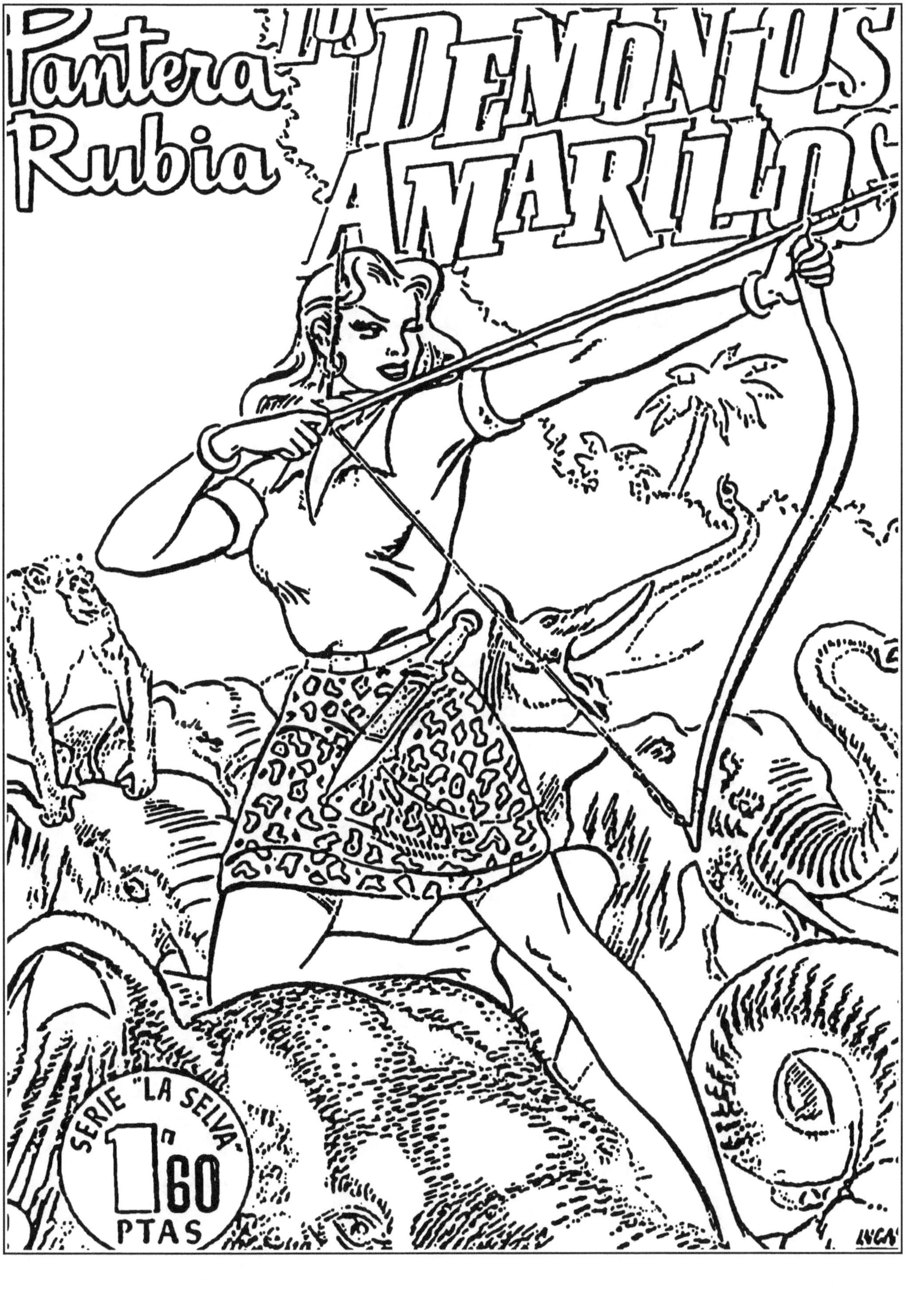
Pantera Rubia
Los
DEMONIOS
AMARILLOS
SERIE "LA SELVA"
1'60
PTAS

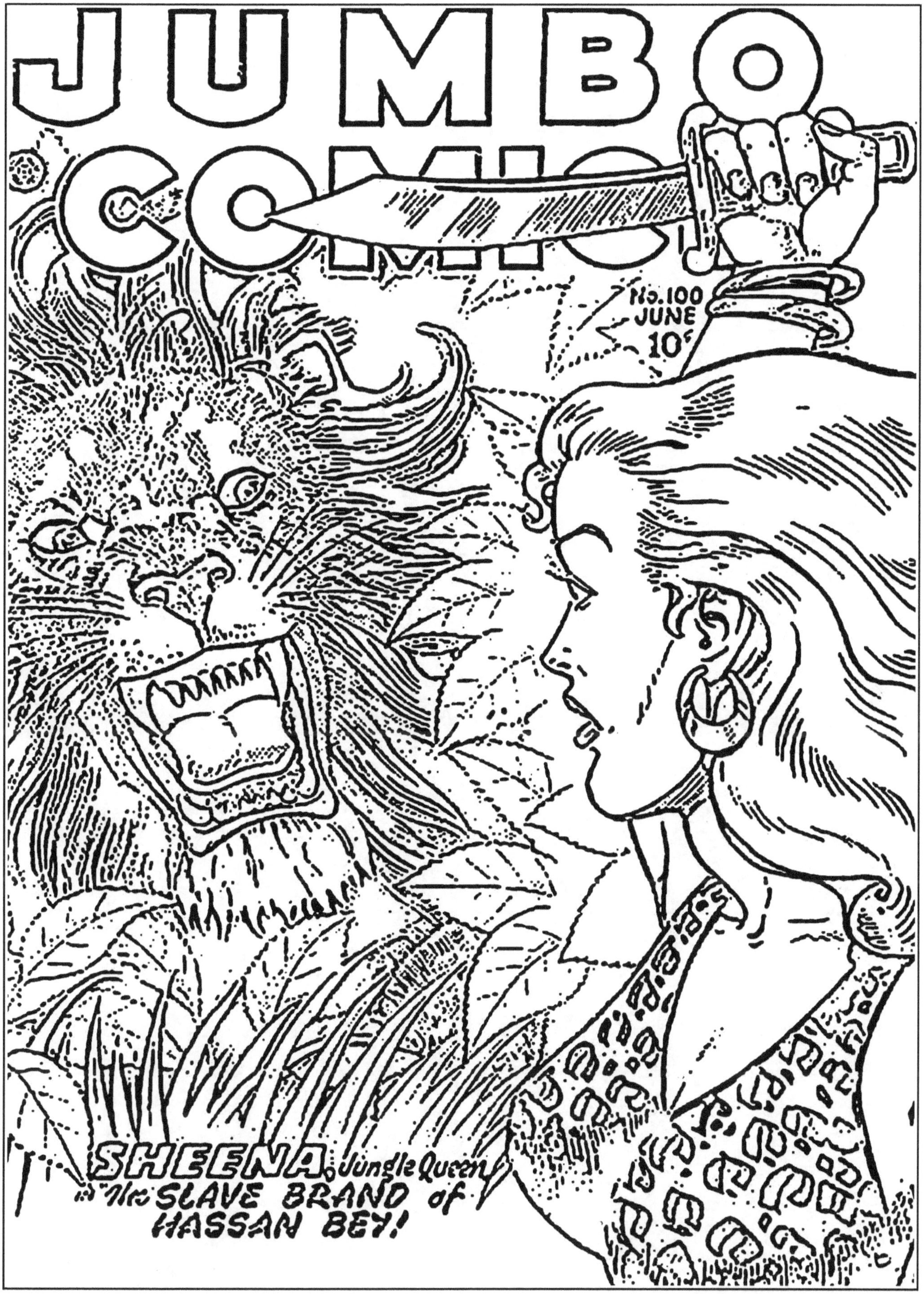
JUMBO COMICS
No. 100
JUNE
10¢
SHEENA, Jungle Queen
in The SLAVE BRAND of HASSAN BEY!

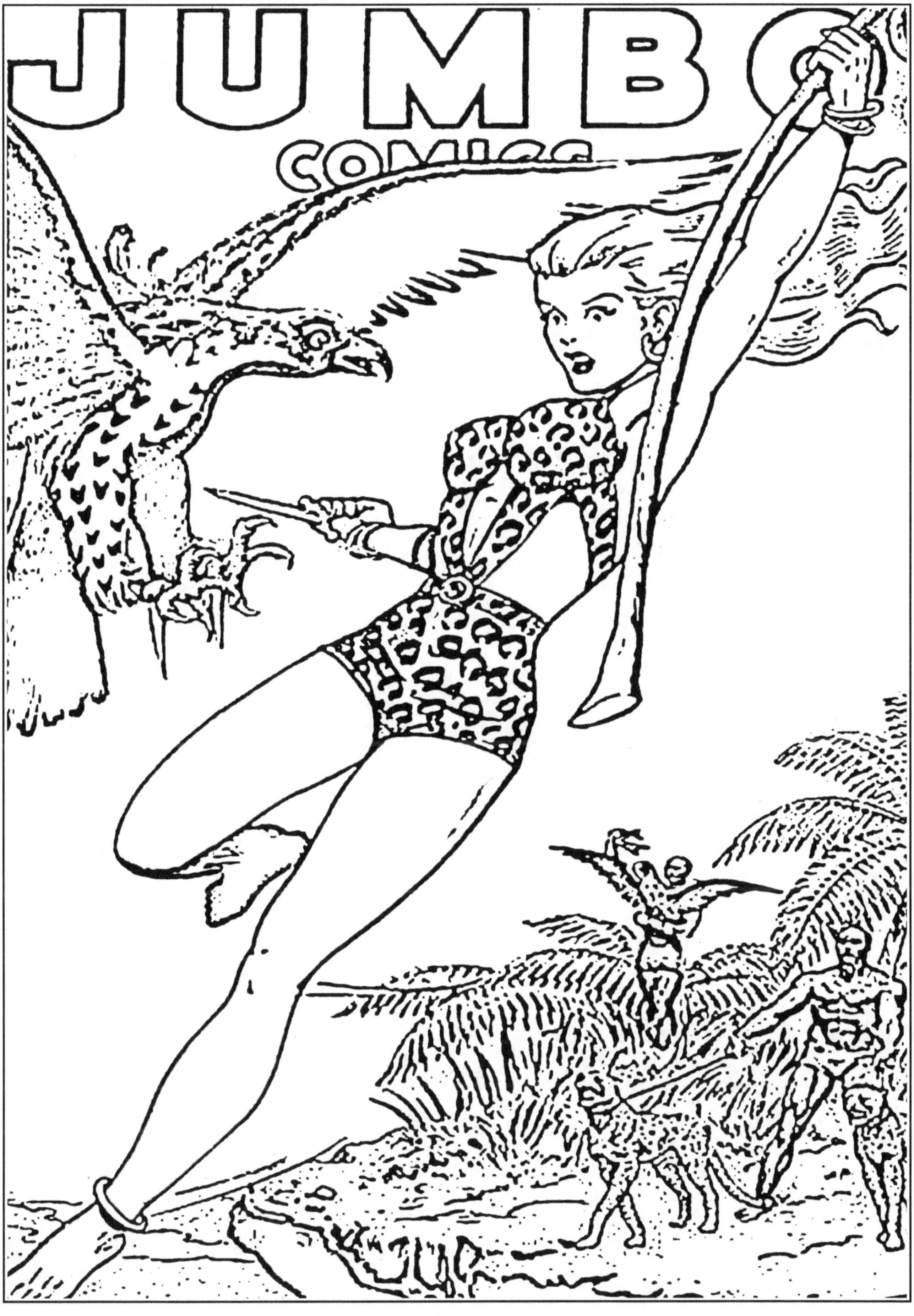
JUMBO

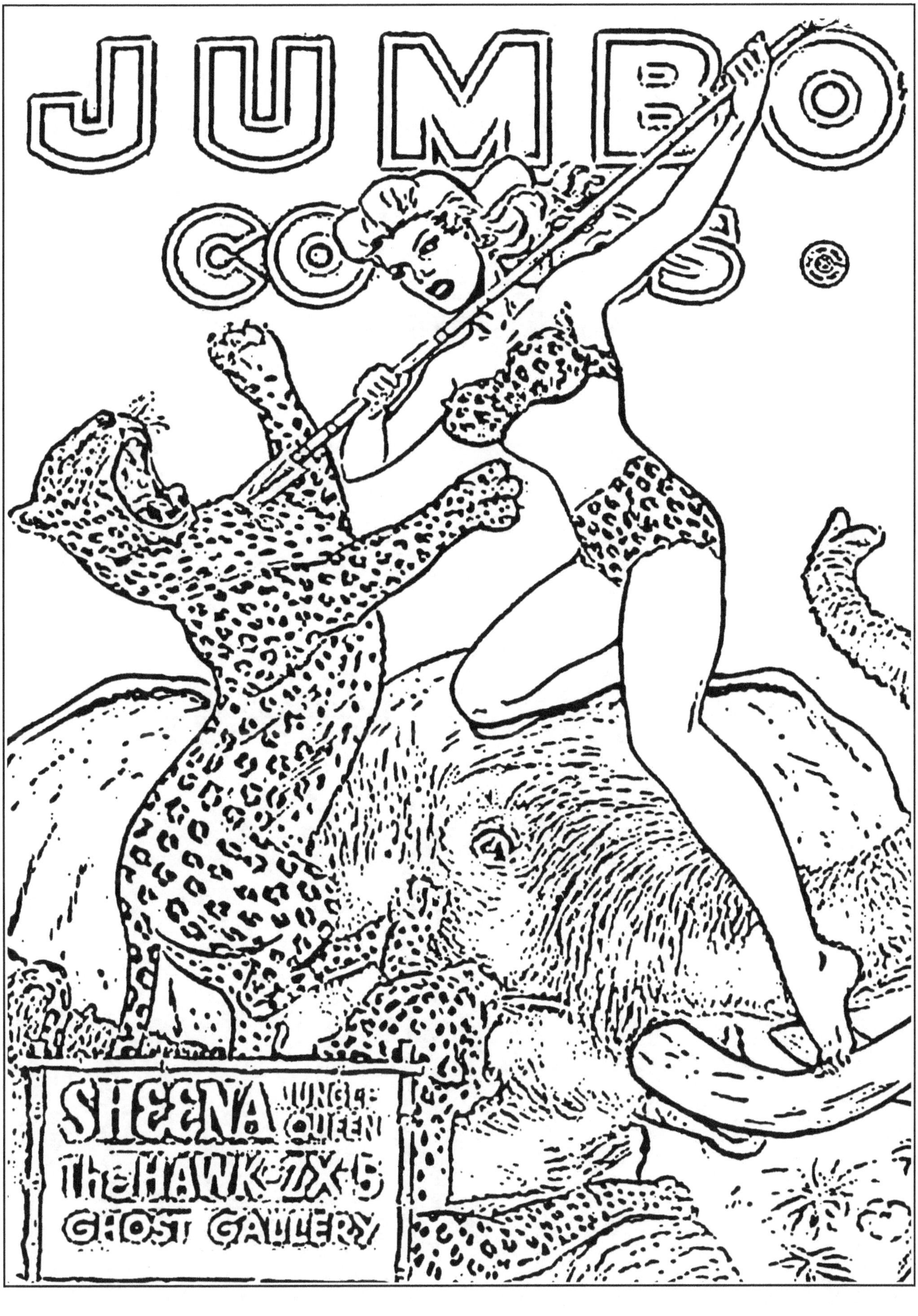
JUMBO
COMICS
SHEENA JUNGLE QUEEN
The HAWK ZX-5
GHOST GALLERY

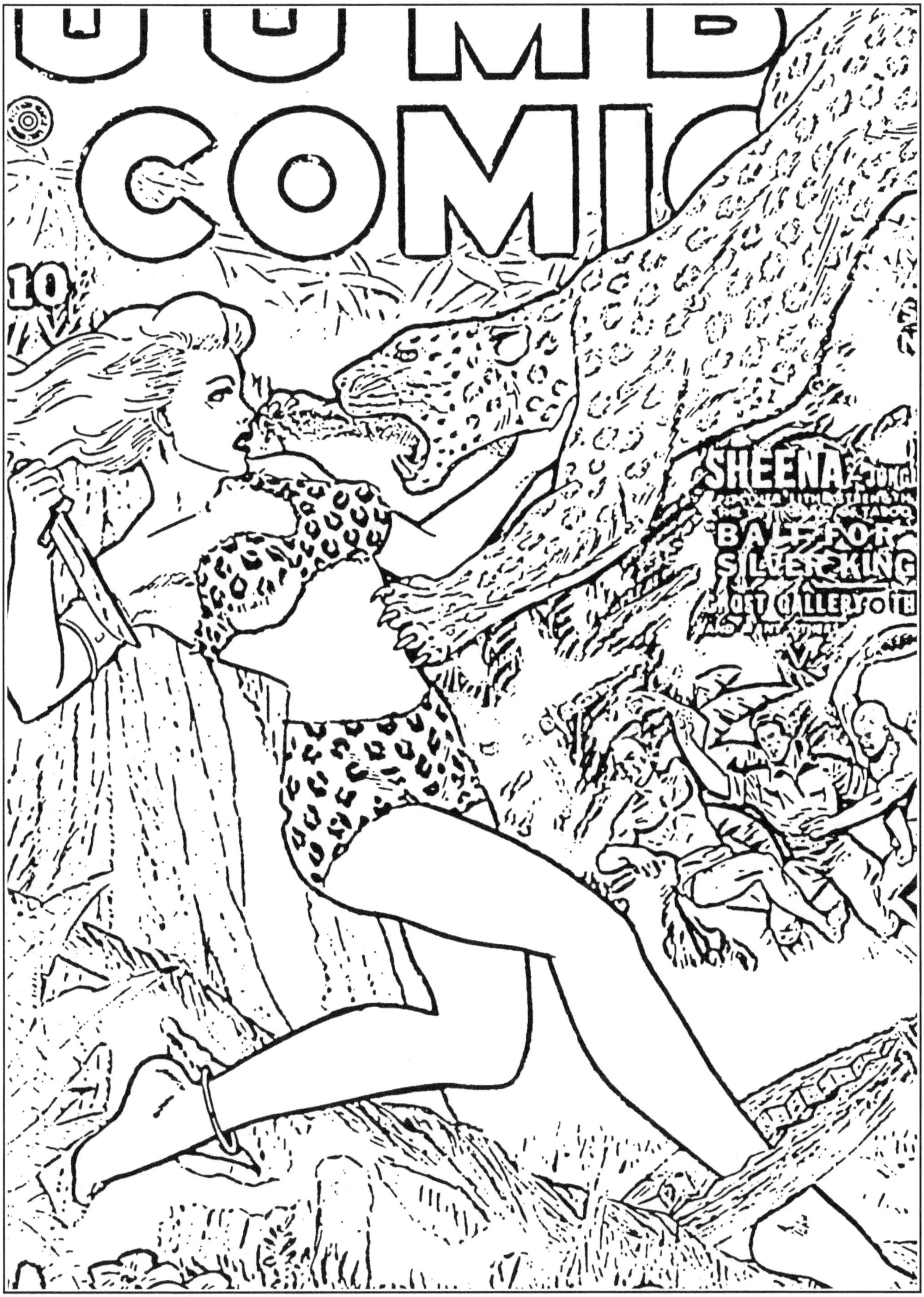
COMIC
SHEENA

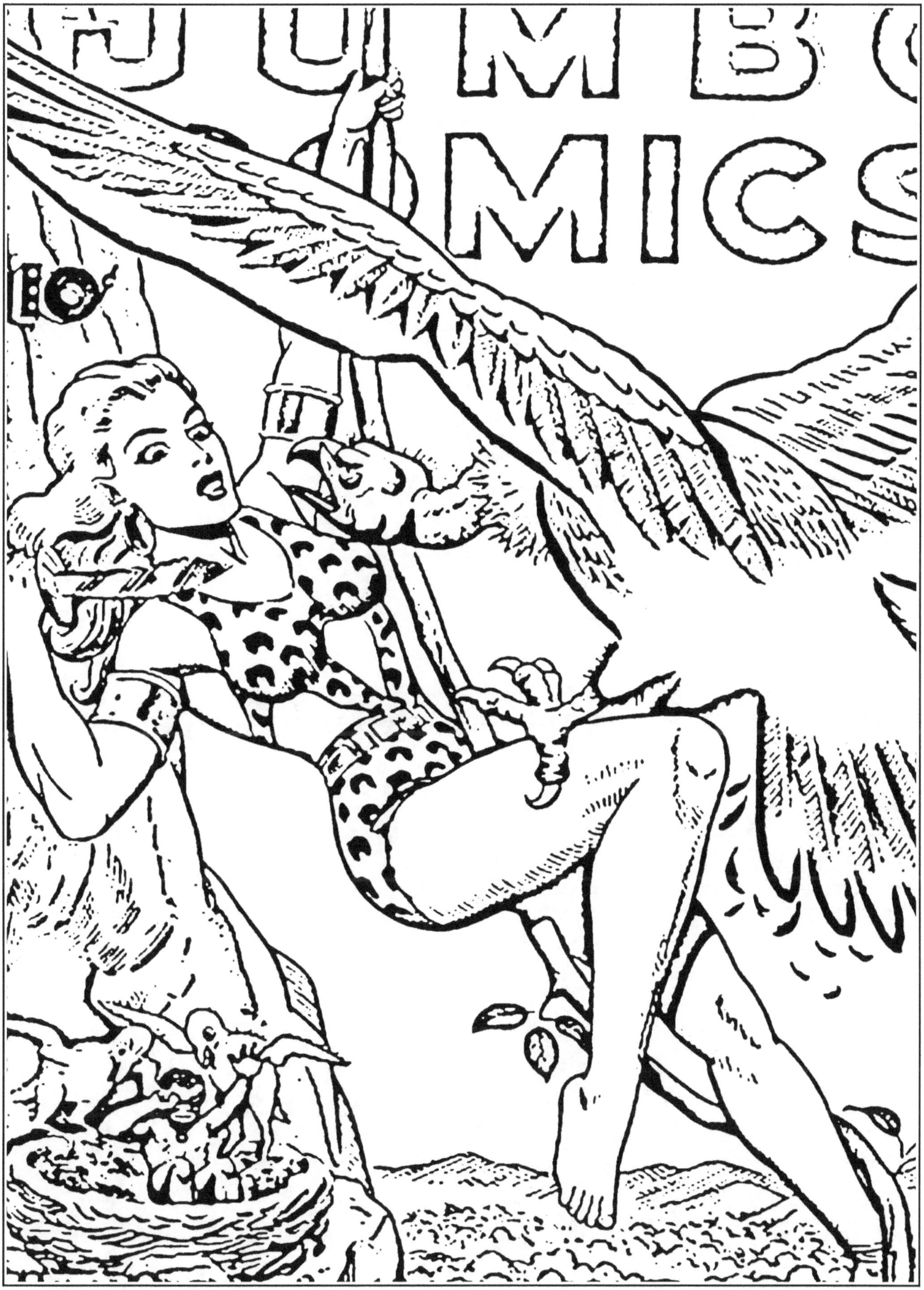

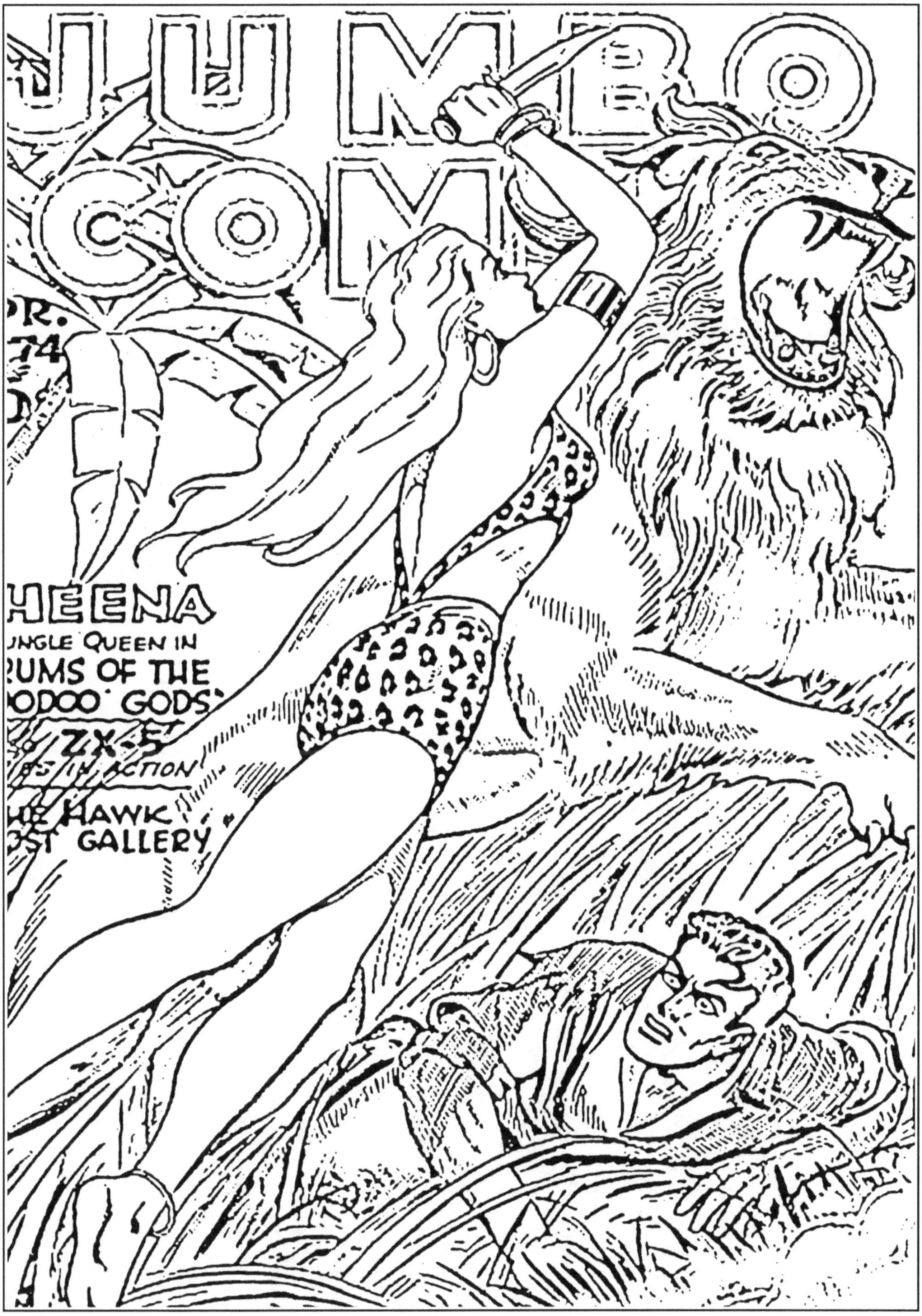

JUMBO
COM
PR.
74
HEENA
UNGLE QUEEN IN
RUMS OF THE
ODOO GODS
ZX-5
IN ACTION
HE HAWK
OST GALLERY

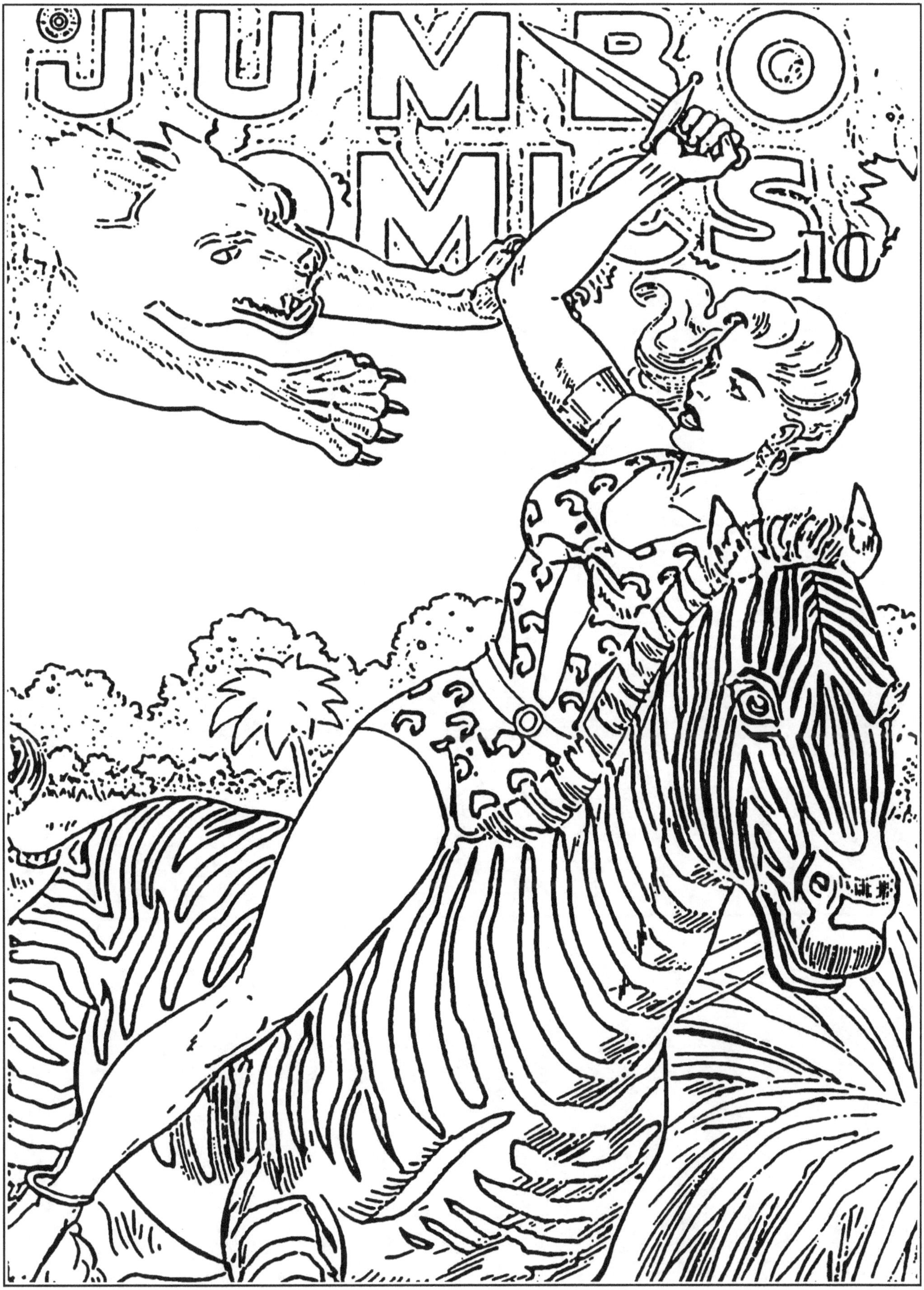
JUMBO
OMICS
10

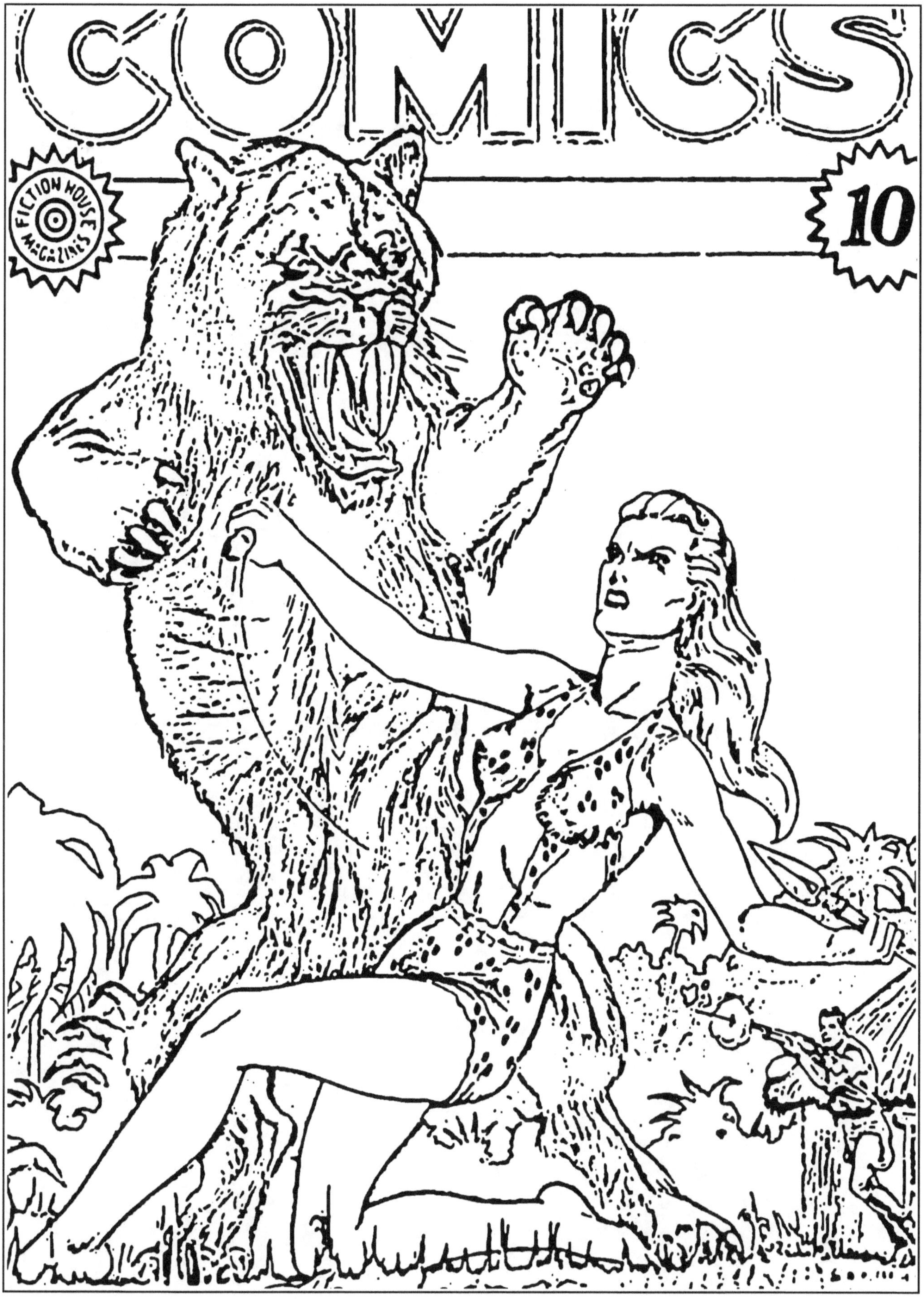
COMICS
FICTION HOUSE MAGAZINES
10

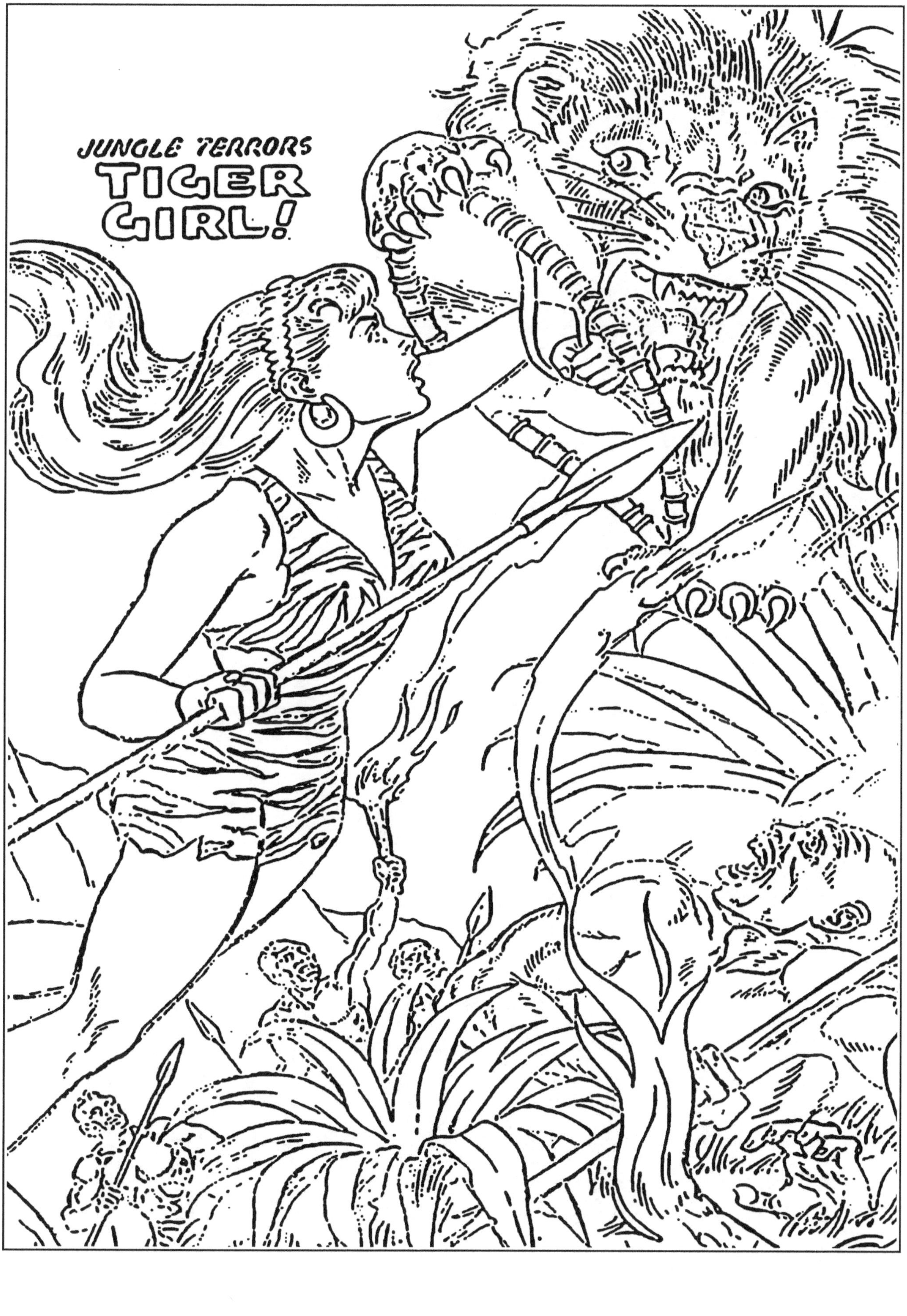
JUNGLE TERRORS
TIGER GIRL!

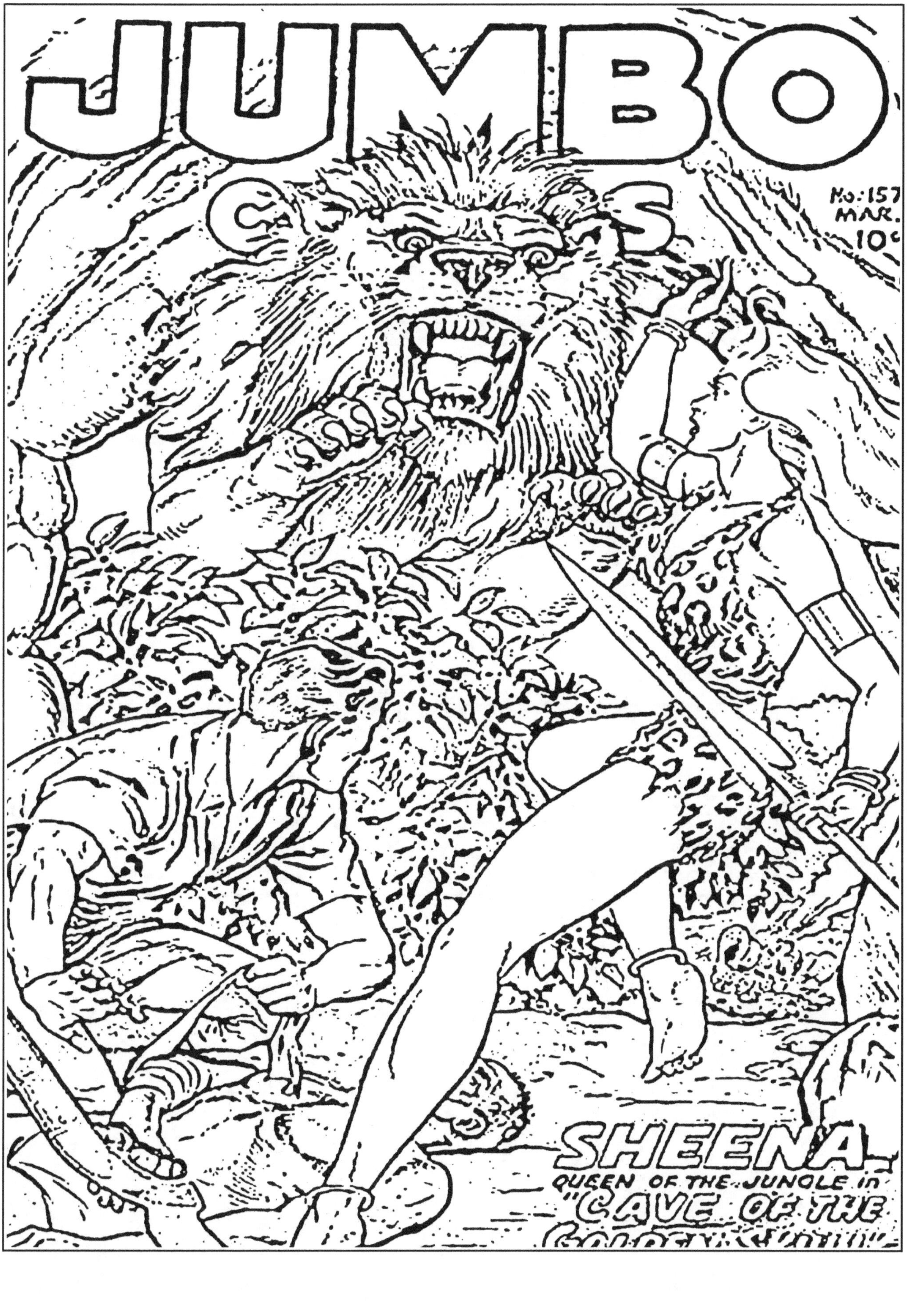
JUMBO
No. 157
MAR.
10¢
SHEENA
QUEEN OF THE JUNGLE in
"CAVE OF THE

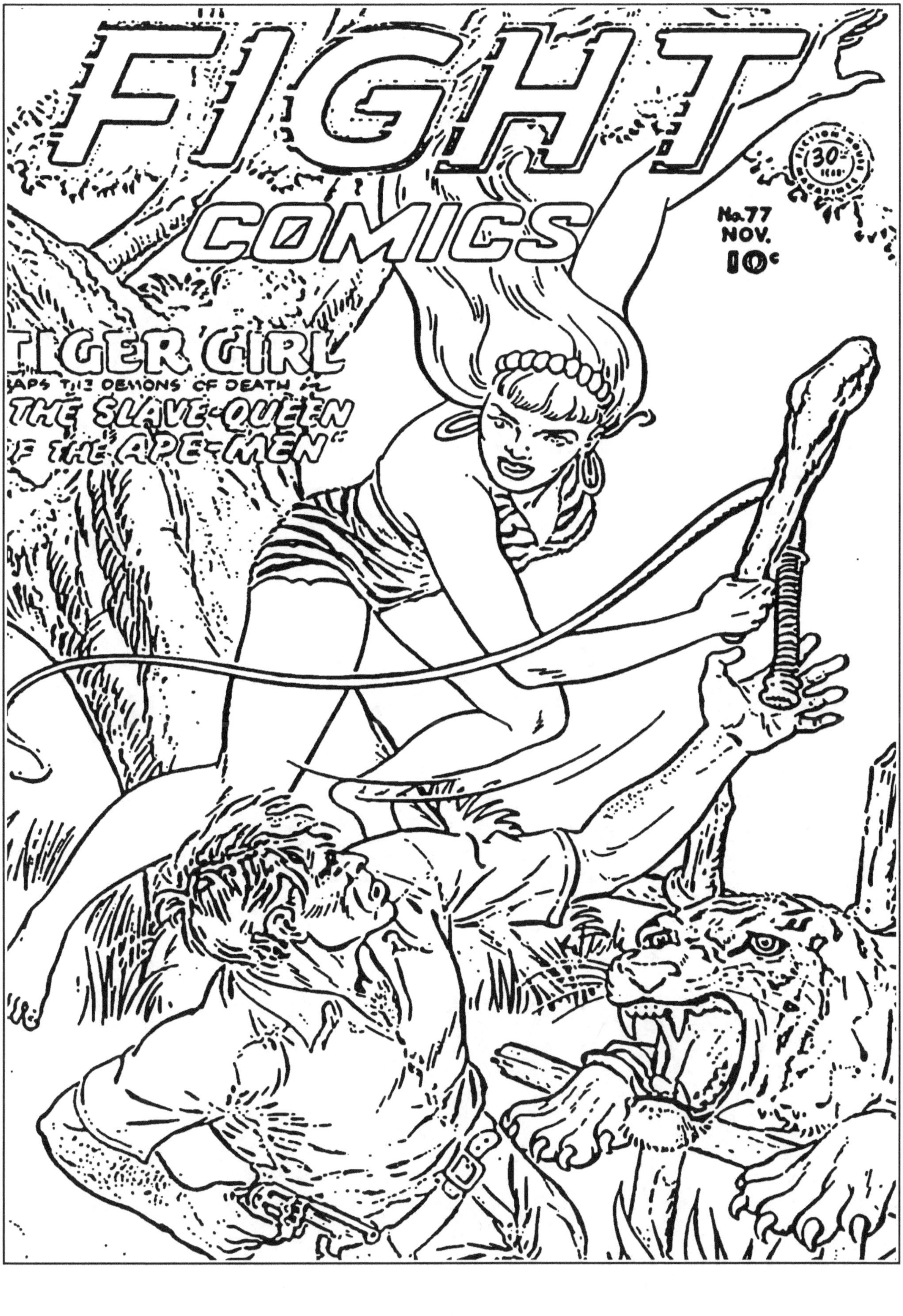

FIGHT
COMICS
No.77
NOV.
10¢
30¢
IGER GIRL
APS THE DEMONS OF DEATH in
THE SLAVE-QUEEN
F THE APE-MEN

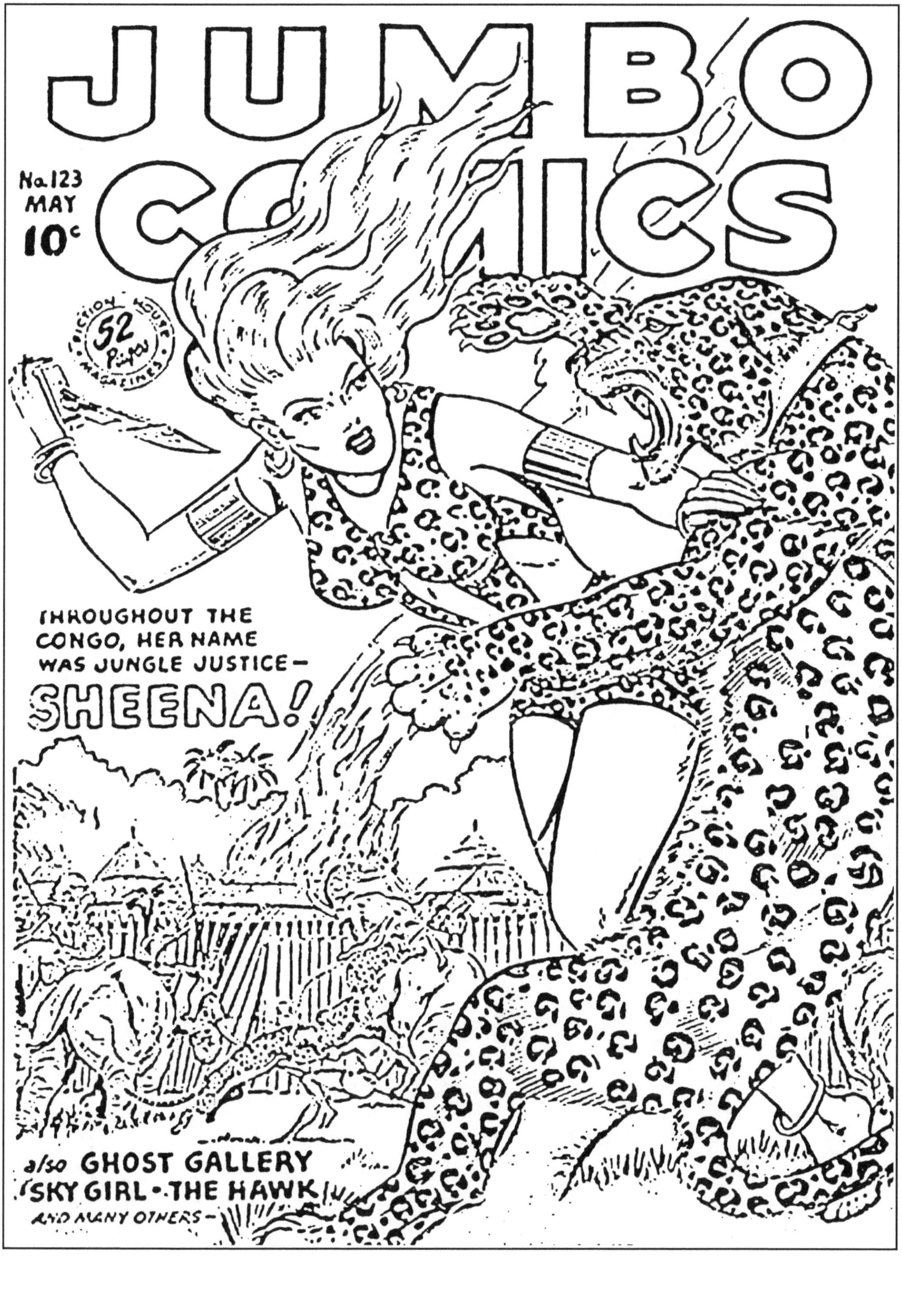

JUMBO COMICS
No. 123
MAY
10¢
FICTION HOUSE
52 Pages
MAGAZINES
THROUGHOUT THE CONGO, HER NAME WAS JUNGLE JUSTICE—
SHEENA!
also GHOST GALLERY
SKY GIRL • THE HAWK
AND MANY OTHERS—

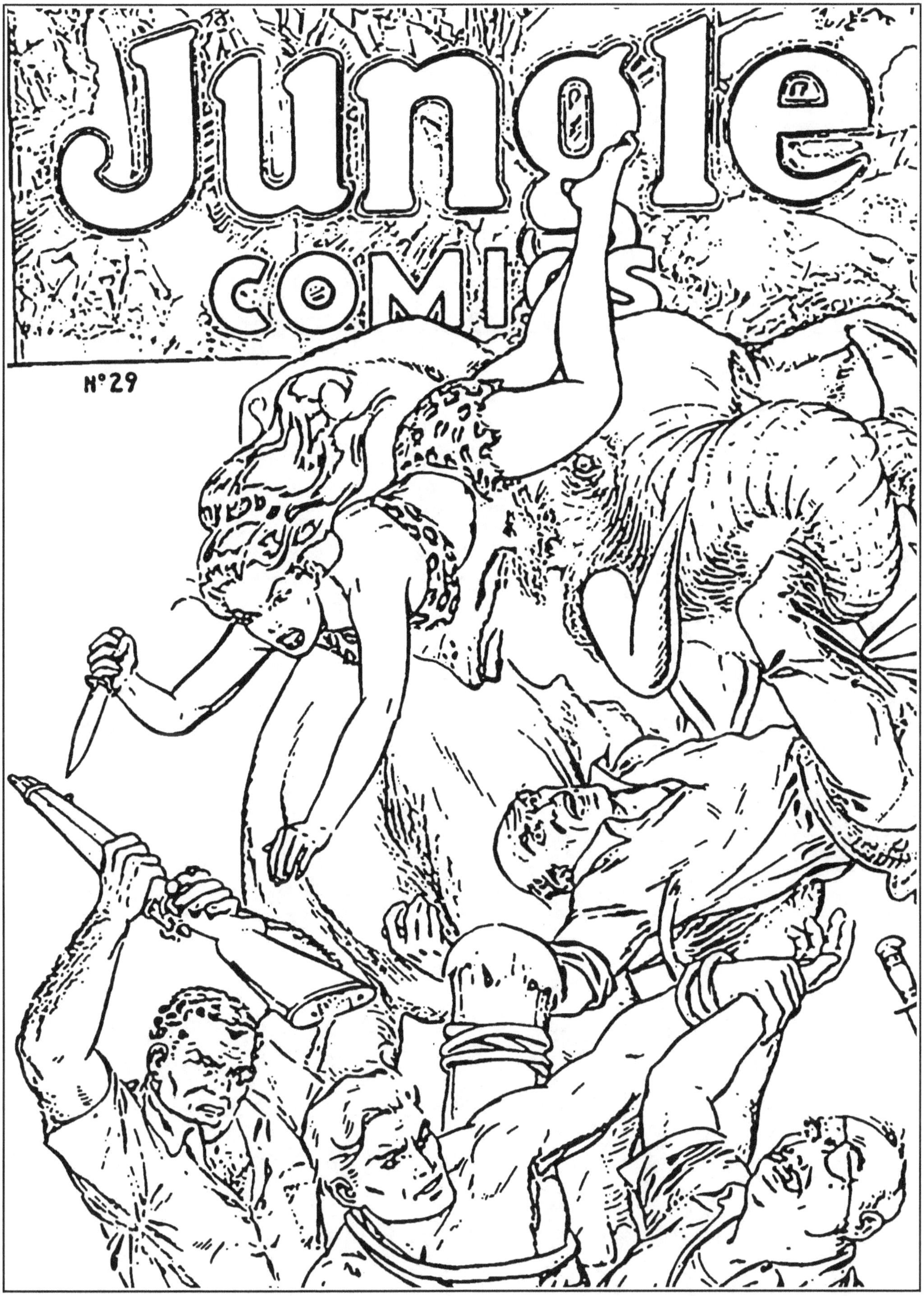
Jungle
COMICS
N°29

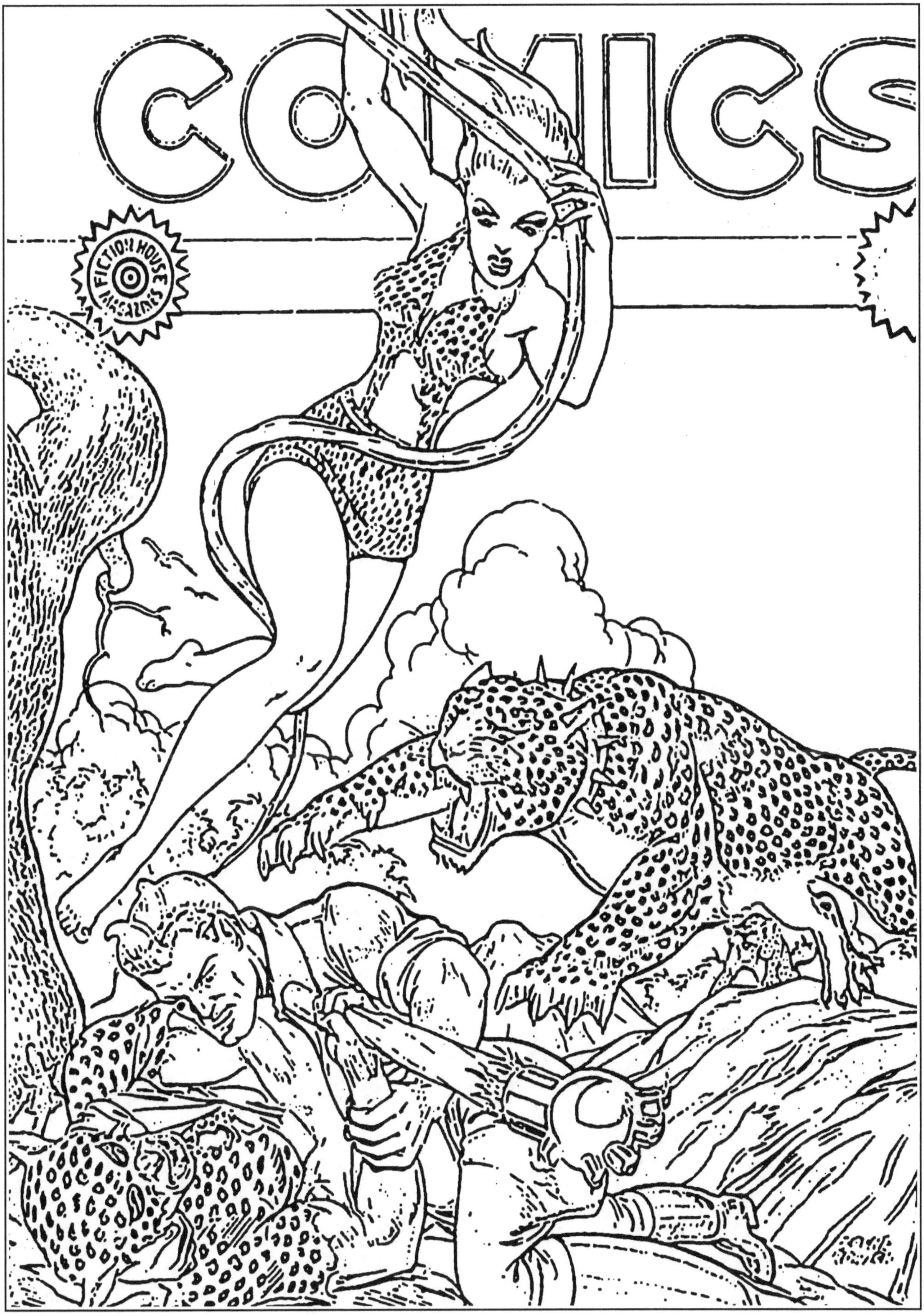
COMICS
FICTION HOUSE MAGAZINES

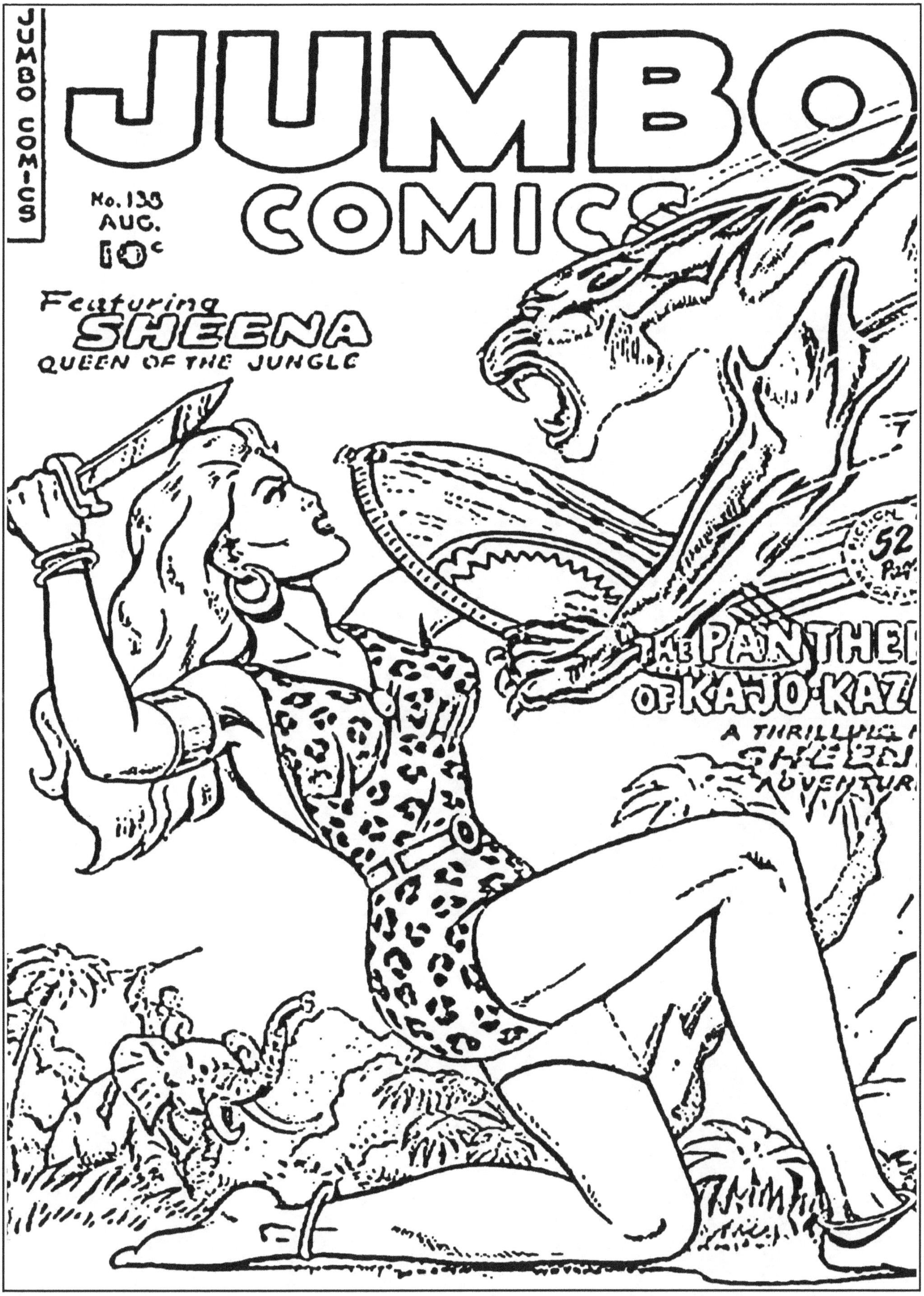
JUMBO COMICS
JUMBO
COMICS
No. 133
AUG.
10c
Featuring
SHEENA
QUEEN OF THE JUNGLE
THE PANTHE
OF KAJO-KAZ
A THRILLING
SHEEN
ADVENTUR

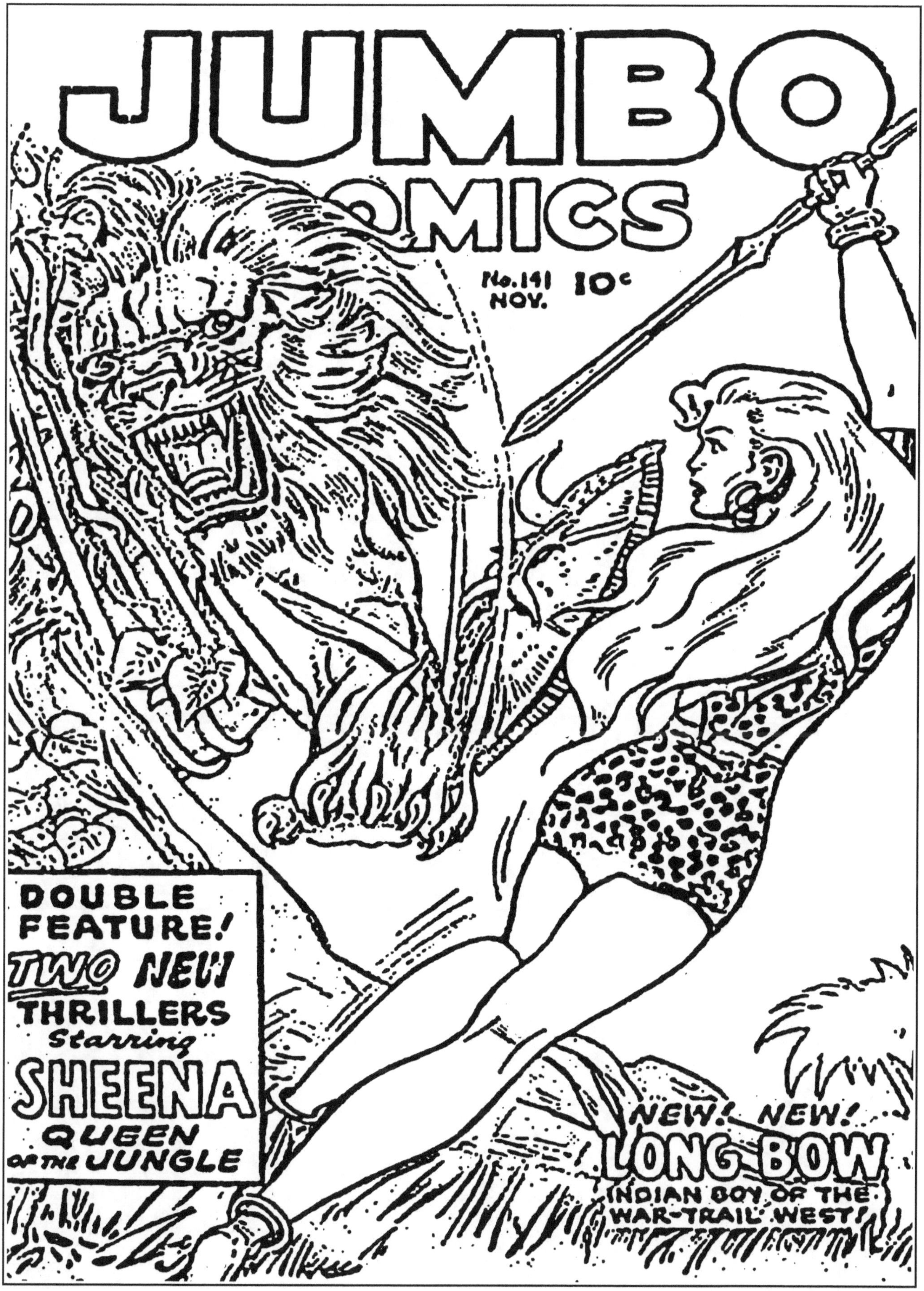
JUMBO COMICS
No.141 NOV.
10c
DOUBLE FEATURE!
TWO NEW THRILLERS
Starring
SHEENA
QUEEN OF THE JUNGLE
NEW! NEW!
LONG BOW
INDIAN BOY OF THE WAR-TRAIL WEST!

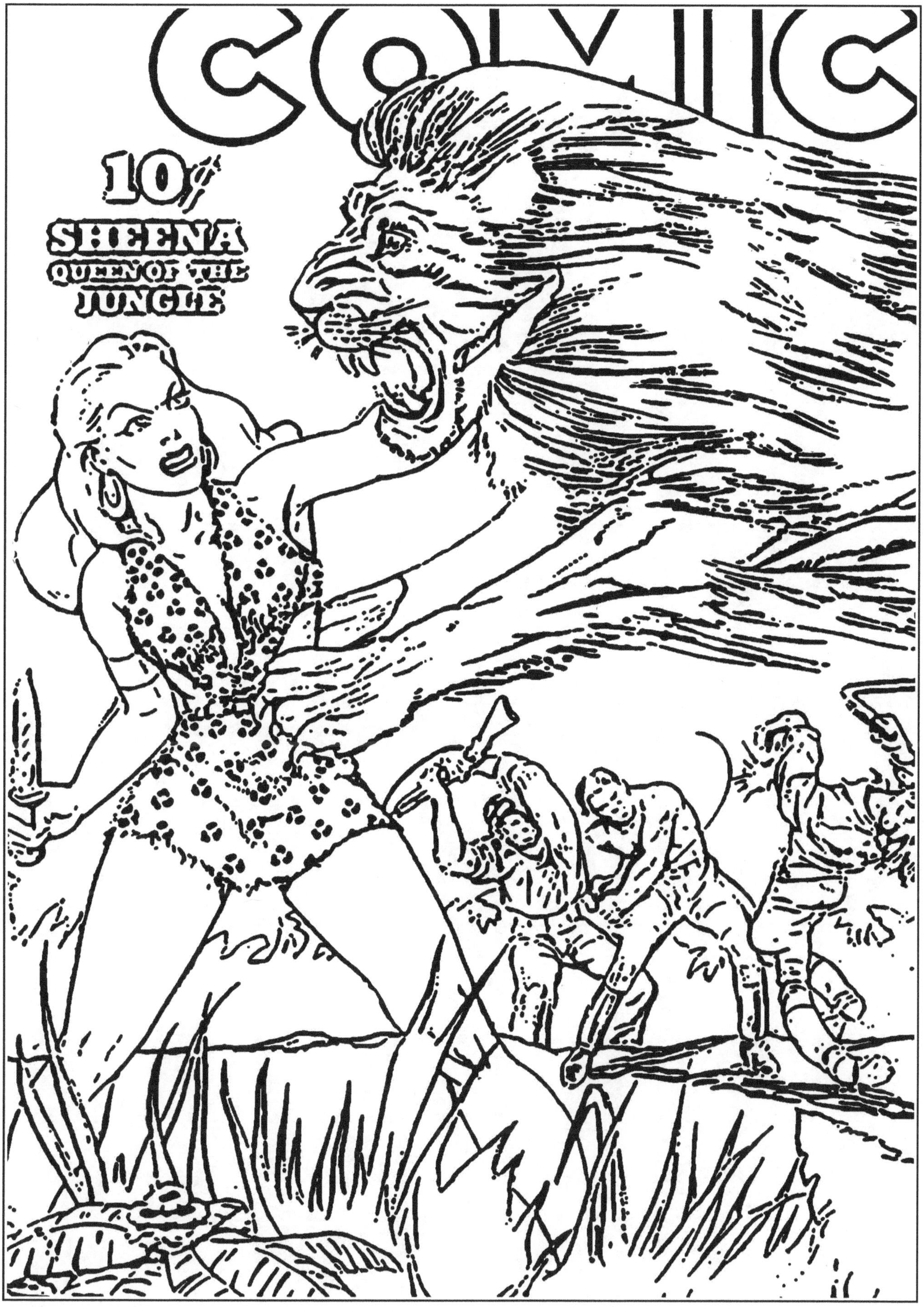
COMIC
10¢
SHEENA
QUEEN OF THE
JUNGLE

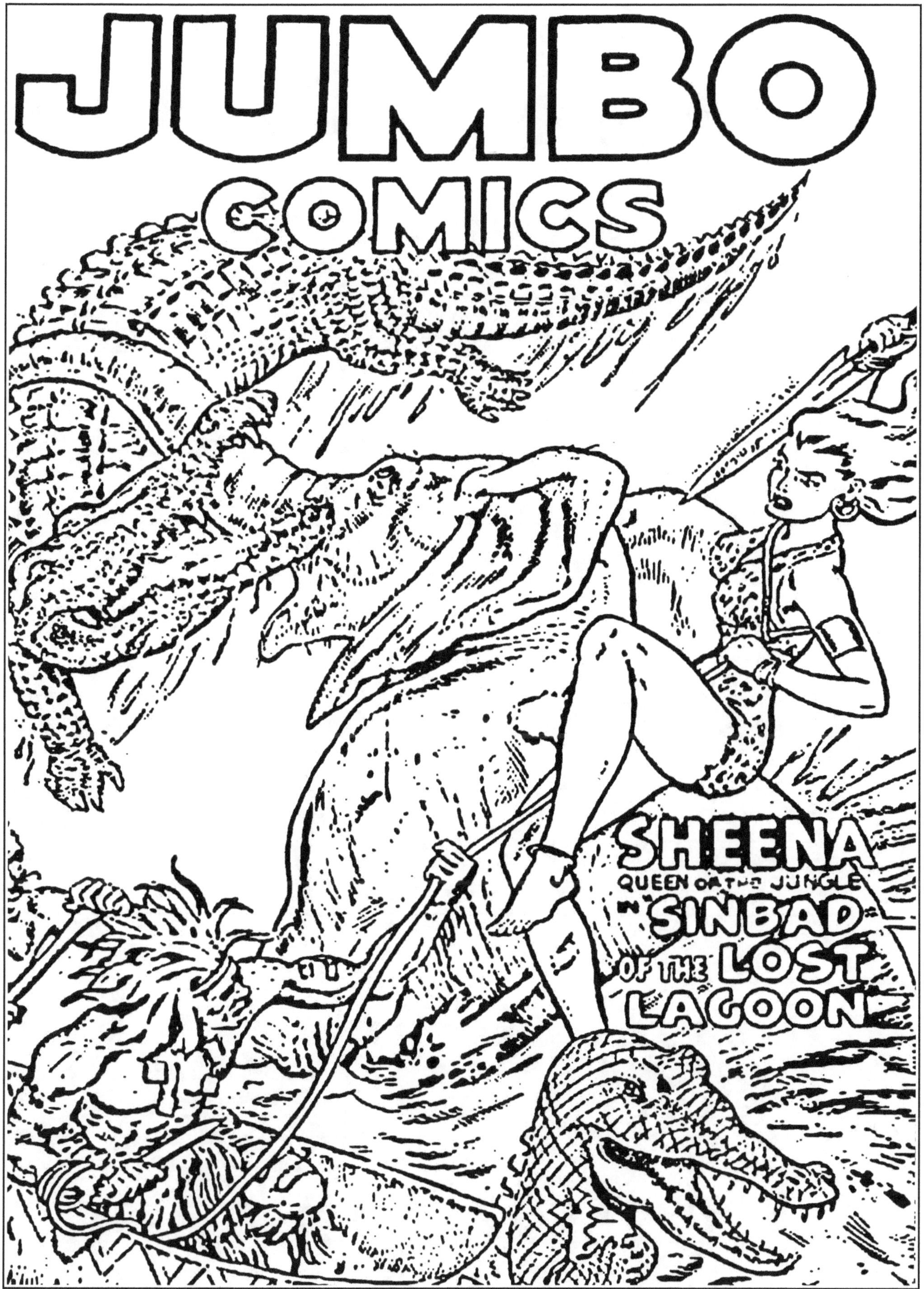
JUMBO
COMICS
SHEENA
QUEEN OF THE JUNGLE
IN "SINBAD
OF THE LOST
LAGOON"

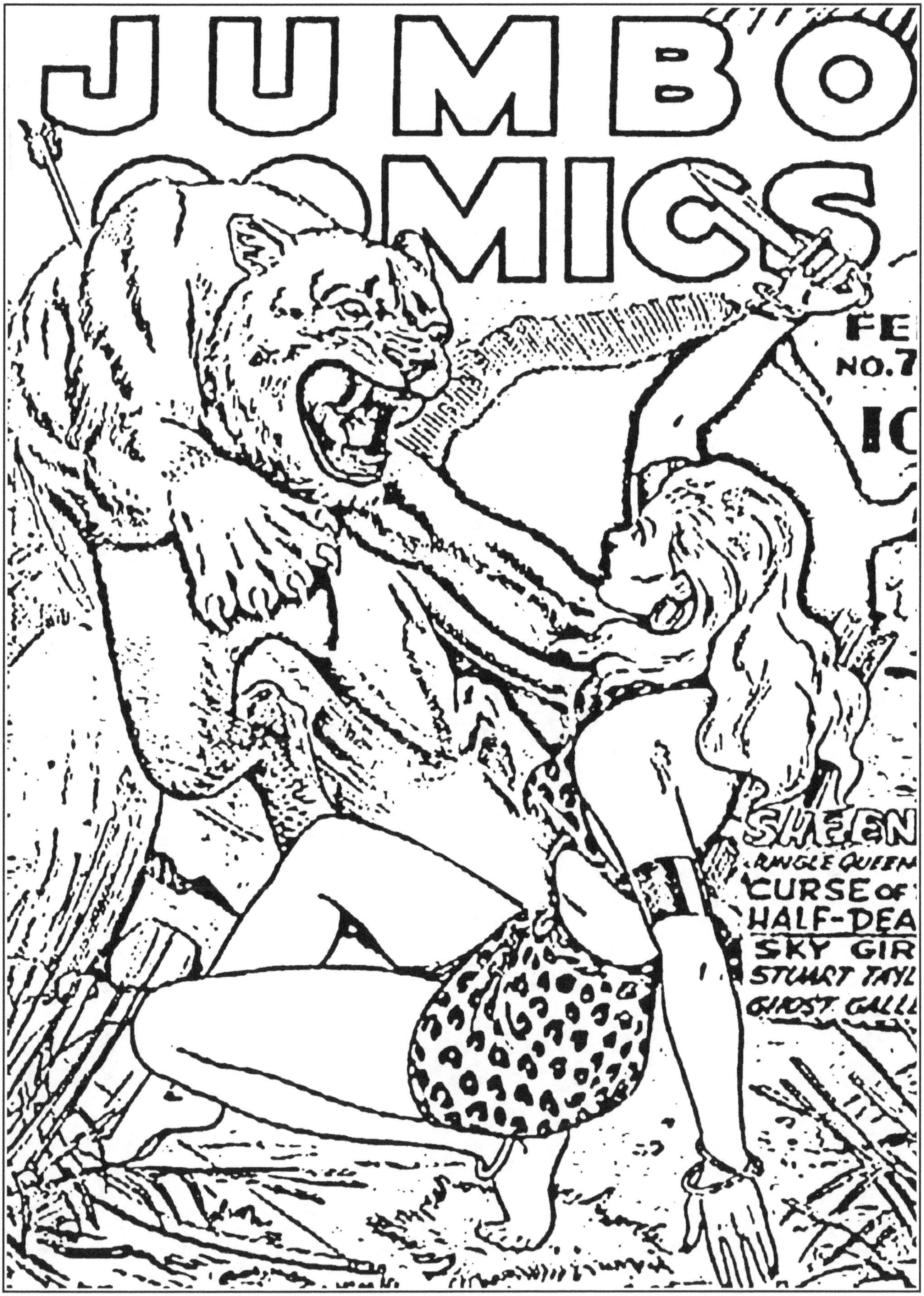

JUMBO
MICS
FE
NO.7
1C
SHEEN
JUNGLE QUEEN
CURSE OF
HALF-DEA
SKY GIR
STUART TAYL
GHOST GALL

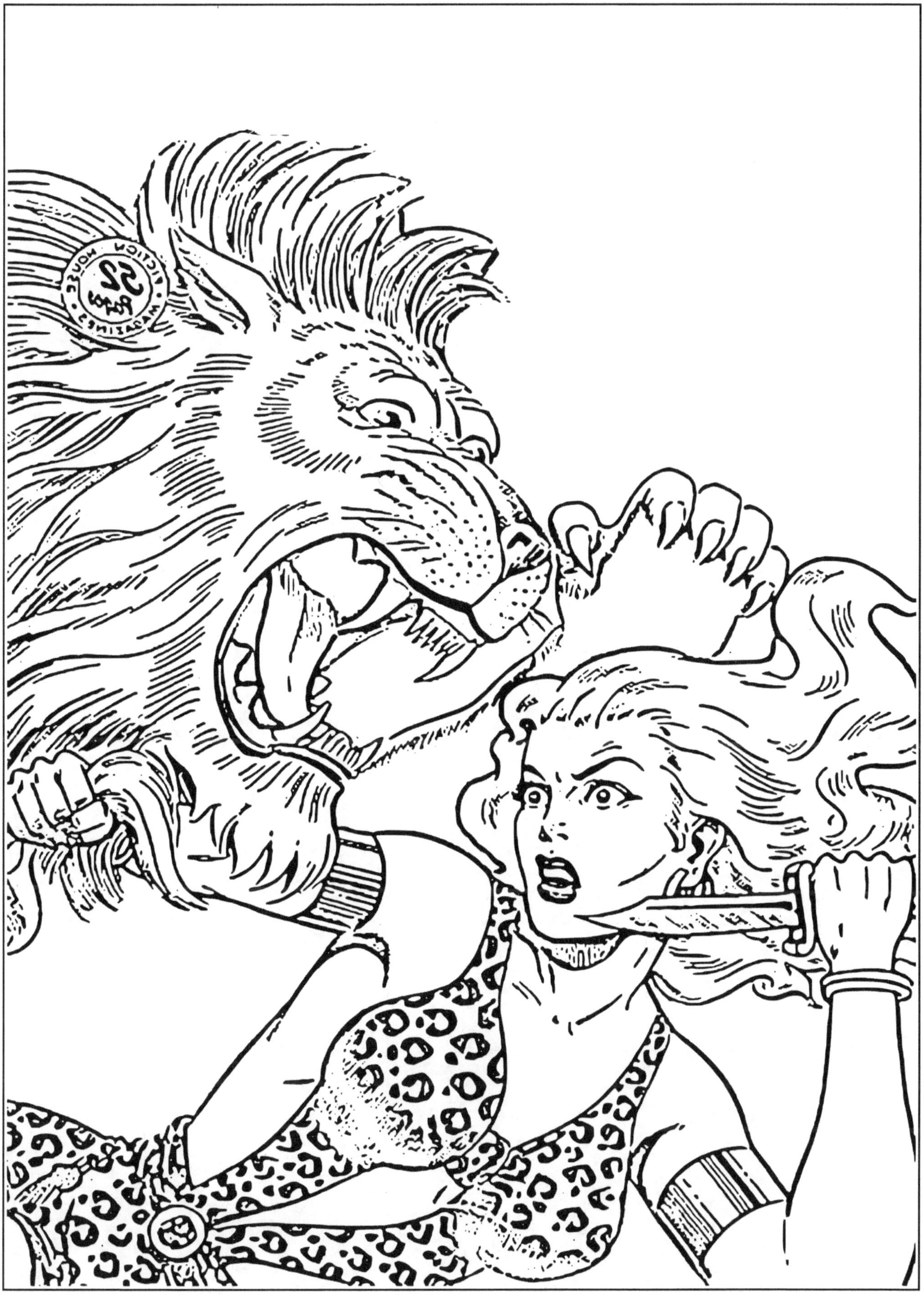

www.ingramcontent.com/pod-product-compliance
Lightning Source LLC
Chambersburg PA
CBHW080636190526
45169CB00009B/3407
* 9 7 8 1 5 3 4 9 1 3 6 0 8 *